Huntingdon Area
Middle School Library
Huntingdon, Pa.

Class No. Acc. No.
598 13686

THE OSTRICH

BY
**WILLIAM R. SANFORD
CARL R. GREEN**

EDITED BY
DR. HOWARD SCHROEDER, Ph.D.
Professor in Reading and Language Arts
Dept. of Curriculum and Instruction
Mankato State University

CRESTWOOD HOUSE
Mankato, Minnesota

LIBRARY OF CONGRESS CATALOGING IN PUBLICATION DATA

Sanford, William R. (William Reynolds).
 The ostrich.

 (Wildlife, habits & habitat)
 Includes index.
 SUMMARY: Describes the physical characteristics, behavior, life cycle, and habitat of the biggest bird in the world.
 1. Ostriches--Juvenile literature. (1. Ostriches.) I. Green, Carl R. II. Schroeder, Howard. III. Title. IV. Series.
 QL696.S9S26   1987   598'.51   87-20175
 ISBN 0-89686-336-0

International Standard Book Number:	Library of Congress Catalog Card Number:
Library Binding 0-89686-336-0	87-20175

CREDITS

Illustrations:
Cover Photo: Leonard Lee Rue III
Stephen J. Krasemann/DRK Photo: 5
Erwin and Peggy Bauer: 7, 9, 15, 18, 40
Leonard Lee Rue III: 10, 17, 43
Joe Cole: 13, 27
Gary Milburn/Tom Stack & Associates: 21, 22
Joseph Berke: 24-25
C. Benjamin/Tom Stack & Associates: 31
W. Garst/Tom Stack & Associates: 34
Bob McKeever/Tom Stack & Associates: 37
Fawcett/Tom Stack & Associates: 38
Andy Schlabach: 45
Graphic Design & Production:
Baker Street Productions, Ltd.

Copyright© 1987 by Crestwood House, Inc. All rights reserved. No part of this book may be reproduced in any form without written permission from the publisher, except for brief passages included in a review. Printed in the United States of America.

Hwy. 66 South, Box 3427
Mankato, MN 56002-3427

13686

TABLE OF CONTENTS

Introduction 4
   Does the ostrich hide its head in the sand?
Chapter One: Birds that can't fly 8
   Some birds stayed on the ground
   A large and varied family
   Adaptations to a flightless life
   Does an ostrich miss flying?
Chapter Two: The ostrich in close-up 14
   Only four subspecies are left
   A walking feather duster
   A body adapted to life on the ground
   A bird that eats everything
   An ostrich depends on its eyes and ears
   Have you ever seen a "camel bird?"
Chapter Three: At home on the African plains 26
   Ostriches are big eaters
   A useful partnership
   Danger from predators
   Chicks and eggs are at risk
   Running and swimming
   Sleeping with heads held high
Chapter Four: A year in the life of the ostrich 33
   A complex nesting behavior
   The eggs hatch
   Leaving the nest
   Fast growth
   A new mating season
Chapter Five: The ostrich is too valuable to lose .. 41
   A craze for ostrich plumes
   Ostrich farms save the species
   Can the ostrich survive?
Map: 45
Index/Glossary: 46-47

INTRODUCTION:

Tom looked upset when he ran into the kitchen. His mother took one look and knew that something had gone wrong at school.

"Do you want to tell me what's on your mind?" she asked.

The story came out in a rush. Tom's teacher had assigned the class reports on wild animals. "By the time it was my turn," he sighed, "the good animals were gone. I got stuck with the ostrich!"

"That doesn't sound so terrible," Mrs. Hansen said.

"Mom, all I know about the ostrich is that it looks like Big Bird on *Sesame Street*," Tom argued.

"Maybe you're not being fair," she said with a smile. "I know a little about ostriches. For one thing, they're the biggest birds in the world. They're so big, they've lost the ability to fly. And when they're scared, they hide their heads in the sand!"

Tom smiled. "Well, that's something," he said. "But I need a lot more facts. To make it worse, the 'O' book is missing from my encyclopedia."

"I know a woman who used to live in South Africa," Mrs. Hansen said. "Why don't you call Mrs. Miller right now? Someone from South Africa is likely to be an expert on ostriches."

Mary Miller laughed when Tom phoned and told her what his mother had said about the ostrich. "Two out

The ostrich is the largest bird in the world.

of three isn't bad,'' she chuckled. "Your mom's right when she says that ostriches are the biggest birds alive. A male ostrich can weigh as much as your mom and dad together. And she's right when she says that ostriches can't fly. Their wings can't lift those heavy critters off the ground!''

Tom looked at his notes. "That's two right,'' he said. "Does that mean ostriches *don't* stick their heads in the sand?''

"They only do that in cartoons,'' Mrs. Miller said. "A real ostrich would never do such a thing. The story probably started in ancient times. A famous Roman writer called ostriches the most foolish of all the birds. He said they thought they were hidden if their heads were out of sight. In time, the idea of 'sticking your head in the sand' became a folk saying. It means that fools think a problem will go away if they ignore it.''

"Well, how does the ostrich hide?'' Tom asked.

"An ostrich looks awkward, but it can usually run away from danger,'' Mrs. Miller explained. "The 'head in the sand' idea probably started when someone saw an ostrich sitting on its nest. The bird can't leave its eggs, so it lays its neck and head flat on the ground. From a distance, the ostrich looks like a clump of grass or a mound of dirt.''

"That's a good story,'' Tom said happily.

"I have some books about African animals,'' Mrs. Miller said. "Ask your dad to pick them up on his way home.''

Tom was waiting when his dad came home from work. "Did you get the books?" Tom asked. "Tonight, I'm going to write a report about ostriches!"

This ostrich wouldn't think of putting his head in the sand.

CHAPTER ONE:

Birds are among nature's most beautiful creations. From tiny hummingbirds to great eagles, these flying miracles fill us with admiration. People have long enjoyed watching their swift, sure flight.

Naturalists believe that the first birds appeared many thousands of years ago. Fossils show that the early "birds" were really small flying reptiles. The archaeopteryx, for example, had teeth and a bony tail. It didn't have fully formed wings, but it did have feathers. In time, these reptile-birds gave way to true birds. Along with wings and feathers, true birds have beaks, two legs, and a high body temperature. They hatch their young from eggs.

Some birds stayed on the ground

Perhaps all early birds were able to fly. Their bodies adapted in many different ways to the demands of a life "on the wing." Naturalists call these birds the carinates. Other birds developed from a similar ancestor, but gave up on flying. These flightless birds are known as ratites. They found ways to survive on the ground or in the water. Even today, their wings still show the same structure as that of the carinates. When it comes to flying,

Birds that can't fly, such as the ostrich, are known as ratites.

however, a ratite's wings are totally useless.

Many ratites have become extinct. Some of these early flightless birds were much bigger than the modern ostrich. The moas of New Zealand, for example, were twelve feet (3.7 m) tall! The elephant bird wasn't as tall, but it was heavier. Naturalists believe that elephant birds weighed as much as one thousand pounds (454 kg). Their huge eggs held two gallons (7.6 liters) of fluids. The skeletons of thousands of elephant birds have been found on the island of Madagascar off the southeast coast of Africa.

Ostriches walk much like humans, placing one foot in front of the other.

Many colorful stories were inspired by the sight of the half-ton elephant bird. In the tales of Sinbad the Sailor, for example, a legendary bird called the giant roc strikes fear into the hearts of all but the bravest. In one tale, a roc swoops down and carries off a full-sized elephant in its talons! That's only a story, of course, but elephant birds were big enough to earn their name honestly.

A large and varied family

The best known and largest of today's ratites is the ostrich. In many ways, ratites such as the ostrich are more primitive than the carinates. Of the twenty-seven orders into which naturalists divide all birds, the ostriches are the second most primitive. Other ostrich-like birds include the rheas of Argentina, the emus of Australia, and the cassowaries of Australia and New Guinea.

Most ratites are large birds, but a few species are no bigger than geese. The kiwis of New Zealand and the penguins of the Antarctic fit into this category. Penguins, which gave up flight in favor of swimming, are the most primitive of birds. The other ratites can swim, but they prefer the land.

Adaptations to a flightless life

Ostriches are typical of most flightless birds. Since they can't fly, their feathers and bodies have adapted to life on the ground. Their feathers are fluffy, like the down on a chick. In addition, ostriches lack the type of breastbone that anchors or holds a carinate's flight muscles. In fact, the name ratite comes from the Latin word for raft. Like a raft, the breastbone of flightless birds is flat.

In choosing running over flight, the ostrich developed long and powerful legs. Horses and other hoofed animals developed into fast runners in much the same way. Instead of developing hoofs, ostriches kept two of their toes. One of the toes supports most of the bird's weight, and has a flat nail. The smaller toe doesn't have a nail.

Most birds hop when they're on the ground. An ostrich walks like a human, one leg at a time. A single giant step can cover up to twelve feet (3.7 m). When the ostrich puts these long steps together, it can reach speeds of forty miles (64 km) an hour for short distances. These world-class runners also "cruise" at thirty miles (48 km) per hour for up to thirty minutes. The ostrich's strong heart makes that type of endurance possible.

Does an ostrich miss flying?

Thousands of years ago, the ancestors of the ostrich adapted to a new way of life. With no need to leave the ground, they lost the ability to fly. When predators tried to catch them, they escaped by running. In its own way, the ostrich became as good at running as a hawk is at flying.

Would the ostrich rather be flying? No one knows. Perhaps it doesn't miss what it has never known.

Does this ostrich want to fly?

CHAPTER TWO:

Naturalists know the ostrich by its scientific name, *Struthio camelus*. Long ago, at least nine subspecies ranged over much of Asia Minor and Africa. Then, as now, ostriches preferred flat, dry plains and grasslands for their habitat. The arrival of farmers and town builders killed off five of the subspecies. The last to go was the Syrian ostrich. It became extinct during World War II. One story says that soldiers ate the last Syrian ostrich.

Only four subspecies are left

The four surviving subspecies of the ostrich live in Africa. Many people call them the African ostrich. Each subspecies, however, varies slightly in size and color.

The endangered Northern ostrich *(Struthio camelus camelus)* is the largest bird alive today. These giants, found mainly in northwest Africa, can reach nine feet (2.7 m) in height. A cock ostrich (an adult male) of that size can weigh 350 pounds (159 kg). A more typical ostrich stands eight feet tall (2.4 m) and weighs 250 pounds (113 kg). The hens (adult females) are a foot (30 cm) shorter and fifty pounds (23 kg) lighter. As much as one-half of an ostrich's height is in its neck and head.

An ostrich hen (left) is shorter and smaller than an ostrich cock (right).

The other subspecies average a foot (30 cm) shorter than the Northern ostrich. The best known is the Masai ostrich *(S. c. massaicus)*. Masai ostriches have pink thighs and necks. They live on the grassy plains of Kenya and Tanzania in east Africa. The remaining subspecies are the Somali ostrich *(S. c. molybdophanes)* and the Southern ostrich *(S. c. australis)*. These two varieties have greyish-blue necks and thighs. The Somali ostrich lives in eastern Kenya, Somalia, and southern Ethiopia. The Southern ostrich is found in southwestern Africa.

A walking feather duster

At first sight, an ostrich looks naked except for its feathery body. Only its thighs and legs are actually bare, however. Covering the neck and head is a coat of fuzzy "hair," made up of hair-like feathers. The cock's egg-shaped body is covered by evenly spaced black feathers. When a cock spreads its wings and tail, the picture changes. Rows of white plumes stand out against the black body feathers. The cock shows off these plumes when it's displaying for a hen. The plumes also make good shade for newly hatched chicks. A young cock sprouts his full adult plumage after his second birthday.

This male displays his plumage in a courtship dance.

As with most birds, the hens lack the male's handsome appearance. Like their newly hatched chicks, the hens wear dull grey-brown feathers. Since they sit on the eggs during the day, their color makes sense. The brown tones help them blend into the dry grasses and sand of their desert habitat.

An ostrich's head is tiny compared to the rest of its body. This cock shows a pink mating flush on its neck.

For its overall size, the ostrich's head is quite small. The large eyes are its most notable feature. Two-inch (5 cm) eyeballs are framed by thick, dark eyelashes. The eyes send signals to a tiny, 1.5-ounce (43 gram) brain. By comparison, a human brain weighs about three pounds (1,361 grams). Another feature of the ostrich's head is a flat, squared-off beak. The beak is made up of several pieces of horn-like material held together by soft skin. Unlike other birds, the ostrich seldom uses its beak as a weapon.

A body adapted to life on the ground

The ostrich's long legs and heavy thighs are bony and muscular. The powerful leg muscles make the ostrich one of the fastest runners in nature. They can kick hard enough to kill a jackal or hyena. The bare thighs also serve as heat radiators. If the day is too hot, the ostrich faces the sun with its wings held out from the body. The wings shade the thighs and allow the release of excess body heat.

In each leg, heavy bones show clearly under the nearly bare skin. What looks like a knee is actually the ostrich's ankle. Of the two toes, the main seven-inch (18 cm) toe supports the bird's weight. Some naturalists believe that the nail on this toe might someday become a hoof. The smaller, outside toe doesn't have a nail. No trace is left in the ostrich's skeleton of the first and second toes found in most birds.

The ostrich's long neck looks delicate, but it's strong and flexible. The bird can stretch up to nip off a tender leaf, or bend down to pick a locust off the ground. The position of an ostrich's neck and head also sends a signal to other ostriches. A bird that stands with head and tail lowered is saying, "I give up." By contrast, a cock with its wings spread, tail up, and neck pushed forward is ready for a fight.

A bird that eats everything

People like to watch an ostrich swallow an apple. The fruit disappears in one gulp. It shows up as a lump that travels the length of the bird's neck. Everything the ostrich eats goes into a three-section stomach that can digest almost anything. Although it eats mostly plants, it likes insects and small animals, too. Its fifty feet (15 m) of intestines do a good job of taking food value from whatever it eats.

Almost from the moment it hatches, an ostrich chick instinctively swallows small stones and sand. These objects stay in a section of the digestive system called the gizzard. The grit and stones help out by grinding tough plant fibers into a more digestible form. Naturalists say that they can tell where an ostrich has been by checking the stones in its gizzard. By matching the various stones to their sources, the ostrich's travels can be mapped. The ostrich is unusual in another way, too. Unlike other birds, the ostrich passes urine separately from its solid droppings.

The main toe (left) supports the ostrich's weight.

An ostrich depends on its eyes and ears

The ostrich depends upon its keen eyes and ears to find food and to warn of danger. With its head twist-

An ostrich can make many different sounds.

ing on the end of its long neck, the ostrich keeps watch in all directions. The smallest movement catches its attention. In addition, although it doesn't have external ears, the ostrich hears quite well. Even while it's alert to the approach of predators, it's also listening for the sounds made by other ostriches. The big bird's senses of smell and taste, however, are poorly developed.

Although wild ostriches don't make much noise, they're far from silent. Their sounds range from pleasant bird calls to harsh snorts and hisses. The cock courts his hens with a mating call that also warns other cocks to stay away. To make this call, the cock closes his beak and forces air down his windpipe. The neck swells like a sausage and makes a muffled roaring sound. Naturalists say this call sounds like the roar of distant lions.

Have you ever seen a "camel bird?"

In ancient times, the ostrich was known as the "camel bird." If that seems like a strange name, look at the bird's long neck, skinny legs, and heavy, rounded body. Except for the lack of a hump, the ostrich does look a little like a camel.

By any name, the ostrich is one of the world's most unusual birds. Its wings and tail are useless for flight. Its neck and legs are too long for its body. Even so, it has survived in its African habitat for thousands of years.

Three ostriches rest in the hot African sun.

CHAPTER THREE:

The sight of a family of ostriches is one of Africa's wonders. The tall cock keeps an eye open for danger while the hens and chicks snap up tender leaves. In the midst of lions and other predators, these flightless birds have made themselves at home.

Ostriches can live wherever they find food, open country, and a warm climate. Except for some small flocks that were shipped to Australia, these big birds live wild only in Africa. There, ostriches are found most often on the dry grasslands known as savannahs. Ostriches also live on sandy plains at the edge of the desert, or in regions of thick bush. If there's enough food, the birds can adapt to life in rocky, hilly areas.

Ostriches are big eaters

The ostrich feeds mostly on grasses, seeds, leaves, and vines. Wild figs or other fruits are a special treat—if it can find them. Along with its plant diet, the ostrich eats insects and small animals. To see an ostrich chasing a mouse is rather comical. The big bird's head darts forward as it zigzags after its prey with quick, awkward strides.

Ostriches swallow sand and pebbles along with their regular diet. The habit is instinctive. They need grit in their gizzards to help their digestion. Naturalists also tell of ostriches getting drunk! If they find a tree full of overripe fruit, the birds will stuff themselves. Then the ostriches will stagger away on wobbly legs.

The grit that an ostrich swallows helps in digesting tough plant fibers.

The plant and animal food that ostriches eat provides some moisture. Ostriches can live for long periods of time if the plants they eat are green and moist. If this isn't the case, however, and they can't find a water hole every few days, they will die of thirst. For that reason, ostriches are experts at finding water. The natives of the Namib desert turn that skill to their own use. Hunters follow ostrich tracks in order to locate hidden water holes.

A useful partnership

Out on the savannah, ostriches often graze near herds of antelope, zebras, or wildebeests. With their height and superior eyesight, the ostriches serve as an early warning sytem. The four-footed animals keep an eye on the ostriches. The sight of an ostrich breaking into a run sounds the alarm. The herd animals don't wait to see if there's really a predator nearby. They turn and run for their lives.

Staying near the herds also helps the ostriches. As the animals move, their hoofs stir up swarms of insects. The ostriches follow close behind, heads down and eyes alert. Each snap of their busy beaks picks a tasty insect out of the air.

Danger from predators

The African plains support many fierce predators. An ostrich makes a good supper for jackals, hunting dogs, hyenas, cheetahs, and lions. The predators are careful around the adults, however. The funny-looking birds can be quite fierce. One direct kick from an angry cock can send a jackal flying. In the same way, a raking blow from a hen's foot can slice open a daring lion cub. When an ostrich is attacked, its mate often comes to its defense.

Along with disease and predators, accidents kill many ostriches. Most of the birds that fall and break their legs will die. If it escapes human and animal predators, however, a healthy ostrich may live sixty years or more. It's not unusual for a forty-year-old hen to hatch a nestful of healthy chicks.

Chicks and eggs are at risk

Of every hundred chicks hatched, only ten will grow to adulthood. Along with the usual predators, birds of prey feed on ostrich chicks if the parent birds are away. But the ostrich has an effective defense against predators. The ostrich cock leads the chicks to safety, while the hen engages the attacker. At other times, the cock takes over. One cock charged a locomotive when he thought the train was a threat to his chicks!

Chicks can hide or run for their lives, but the eggs are always in danger. The eggs incubate in a shallow nesting hole that the cock digs in sandy soil. There's no way to hide them. If a predator comes by, the ostriches will risk their lives to protect their nest. But predators can be tricky sometimes. While the cock and hen are fighting with a lion, another lion may sneak in and scatter the eggs.

Finding ostrich eggs is easy, but eating them is another matter. Each egg is six inches (15 cm) around and weighs up to three pounds (1.4 kg). That's as big as twenty-five chicken eggs! Most lions can't open their mouths wide enough to crush an egg. In addition, the shell is as thick as a china plate. A man can walk on a clutch of eggs without breaking them.

Only a few animals have figured out how to crack ostrich eggs. Naturalists have seen hyenas rolling one egg against another, hoping one will break. The Egyptian vulture has worked out a better system. This clever scavenger throws small stones at the eggs! The vulture holds a stone in its beak and flips it at an egg. The vulture's aim is poor, but it has a lot of patience. After many misses, a direct hit sometimes cracks the egg.

Running and swimming

When frightened, an ostrich zips off at a very high speed. At its top speed, an ostrich can outrun most animals. A lion is a little faster, but an ostrich doesn't tire as easily. After a short chase, the lion usually gives up. These speedy birds can also outrun hunters on horseback. The hunters may still catch the ostrich, however. Driven by instinct, the ostriches run in a great circle.

Ostrich eggs have thick shells and can weigh up to three pounds (1.4 kg).

This gives the hunters a chance to cut them off.

Ostriches are excellent swimmers as well. If the adult birds jump into a water hole, the chicks follow them. The adult birds sink until only their necks and heads are showing. In the hot African desert, a cooling swim can be a lifesaver for a big, feathered bird.

If they can't take a swim, ostriches have another way to clean themselves. The birds look for large, dust-filled holes. Then they lower themselves into the hole and flop from side to side. As they flap and twist, they raise a small dust storm. These "dry baths" clean the ostriches' skin and feathers. The dust also gets rid of skin parasites.

Sleeping with heads held high

Ostriches are most active during the day. At night they settle down and sleep for several hours. They close their eyes when they sleep, but hold their necks upright. During the night, they wake up several times to stand and stretch. In a large flock, some of the birds are always awake.

This alert behavior makes it hard to study the ostrich in its native habitat. The naturalists who watch them must find a way to hide near a nest. One team hid inside a fake termite mound in order to study the ostrich's life cycle.

CHAPTER FOUR:

July brings hot, dry days to Kenya's Nairobi National Park. The grass turns brown and the red earth bakes under a blazing sun. Out in the bush country, a flock of fifty Masai ostriches moves slowly toward a water hole.

Each cock shows a pink mating flush on his neck and legs. He stamps the ground and displays his white plumes in a courtship dance. When a hen accepts him, he leads her away from the flock. The cock and hen may stay together for several years. This hen is called a "major hen." Whenever another male wanders by, the cock hurries to protect his square mile (2.6 sq. km) of breeding territory. His angry roar booms across the plain.

A complex nesting behavior

Ostriches have a complex family life. Because there are more hens than cocks, many younger hens do not find a permanent mate. These "minor hens" wander across several territories, mating with each cock they meet. When they're ready to lay their eggs, they approach any of the nests within a five-mile (8 km) area. After a minor hen lays an egg, the major hen chases her away.

While the hen keeps the eggs from overheating, the cock watches for predators.

Over a period of three weeks, ten minor hens add their eggs to a single clutch. Each straw-colored egg is lightly speckled. The nest now holds forty eggs, too many for the sitting ostriches to cover. The record is ninety-four eggs, counted in a single nest in the Sudan.

It's night, and the cock is taking his turn on the nest. He sits with his feathers fluffed out and his neck curved in an alert U-shape. When the sun comes up, the major hen takes his place. If both birds leave the nest, they cover the eggs with sand.

As the day heats up, the hen's body keeps the eggs from overheating. Today she pushes the extra eggs into small pits outside the nest. Some naturalists believe this slows down the growth of the chicks inside the eggs. Others say that these eggs are almost always those laid by the minor hens. They think the hen does this so that predators will be more likely to eat another hen's eggs. In the days to come, the sun kills some unhatched chicks by "cooking" the uncovered eggs.

The eggs hatch

October brings the first rains of Kenya's short wet season. Tender grass blades sprout across the plain. On the forty-second day after the last egg was laid, hatching begins. Somehow, the chicks have developed at the same rate, so that all hatch within a day or two.

For a week now, the adult ostriches have been making clucking noises to the eggs. Tiny peeps answer them from inside the eggs. By the time they hatch, the chicks will know the sound of their parents' voices. The process by which newly hatched chicks learn to recognize their parents is called imprinting.

One of the chicks pushes hard against the inside of the thick shell. A small window breaks open with a popping sound. The chick rests, tired out by its struggle. Then it gives one last shove and the egg splits apart.

One by one, eighteen other eggs break open. The bright-eyed chicks are wearing coats of spiky grey-brown down. For a while, they huddle in the nest, peeping softly. Each is twelve inches (30 cm) tall.

Leaving the nest

Within a few hours, the chicks leave the nest. Their first shaky steps soon become more confident. The chicks peck at everything. Each one swallows some small pebbles. Instinct tells them that they need the stones to help them digest their food. When they're strong enough, the cock leads them away to find food.

The chicks learn to listen for the calls made by the adult birds. They come running when the cock gives a call that sounds like "boo!" That same call, when made twice, means "danger!" Instantly, the chicks lie down and stretch their necks flat on the ground. From a distance, they look like small bundles of weeds.

A hyena trots by, looking for a dinner of ostrich chick. The cock gives the signal and the chicks freeze. Like most predators, the hyena doesn't notice prey that isn't moving. But the cock isn't taking any chances. He runs in circles and drags one wing as if he's wounded. The hyena rushes at the "wounded" bird. Quickly, the cock runs off, staying just out of reach. The hyena dashes after its prey, but the ostrich runs back and forth. Finally, the hyena tires of the chase and gives up. When the cock sounds "all clear," the chicks jump up and scamper back to him.

Fast growth

By the time they're four weeks old, the leggy young ostriches can run up to thirty-five miles (56 km) per hour. They're growing at a rate of nine inches (23 cm) a month. The chicks are still easy prey, however. Of the nineteen that hatched, seven have been killed by predators.

If they're not ordered to freeze when danger is near, the chicks race off in all directions. During one brush with a pack of jackals, three of the chicks get lost.

A young ostrich takes its first shaky steps.

By the time they're a year old, ostrich chicks can find food and defend themselves.

Luckily, they find a cock that likes orphans. He adds the lost chicks to a flock that already numbers over seventy.

The dry season makes food harder to find. The cock decides it's time to join his flock with those of several other males. When he's by himself, the cock must spend thirty-five percent of his day watching for danger. That cuts down on his feeding time. By joining a flock, he reduces his "guard duty" to fifteen percent of the time.

The months pass. At one year, the chicks form a subflock with others their age. The young cocks are almost as big as the adult birds. They can find food and defend themselves. The cocks flap their wings and spread their tails to show off their first white plumes. Next to them, the young females look colorless.

A new mating season

When they're three years old, the cocks are ready to mate for the first time. One strong young cock has chosen a plump hen for his mate. The two sleep near each other. Each day, the hen follows the cock in his hunt for food.

An older cock tries to cut in on the young hen. The young cock's face flushes bright red. He rushes toward the older bird, wings outstretched. The older cock isn't ready for a fight. The young cock chases him away,

After mating, a cock and hen may stay together for several years.

snorting angrily. Then the young male returns to his mate with his head held high.

In July, the cock leads the hen to a nesting spot. He throws himself down and beats his wings against the ground. The dust flies as he hollows out a nest bowl. The hen circles around him, dragging her wings. Then the cock jumps up, still beating his wings. He whirls and dips, his booming cry echoing across the plain. The female crouches on the ground, ready to mate. The age-old life cycle of the ostrich is about to begin.

CHAPTER FIVE:

Most ostriches aren't afraid when they see a jeep drive by. Living on a game preserve, they've lost their fear of people. At one time, however, the humans who now protect them were driving these great birds toward extinction.

Thousands of years ago, early man carved pictures of ostriches in sandstone. These early hunters killed the big birds for food and plucked the plumes for decoration. To the Egyptians, the plumes became a symbol of equal justice. Unlike the feathers of other birds, the vanes on each side of an ostrich plume are exactly the same length.

In South Africa's Kalihari desert, the gentle bushmen still collect the shells of broken ostrich eggs. In the desert, the hard, thick shells are precious. The bushmen use them as bowls to hold the dew they collect from plants. In addition, the women of the tribe wear beautiful jewelry made from the shells.

A craze for ostrich plumes

People hunted the ostrich for centuries, but it was never in danger of becoming extinct. That changed in the 1800's, when ostrich feathers became a fashion craze. Women wore them in their hair and carried ostrich-feather fans. Others arranged the plumes in bouquets. Some people cleaned their homes with feather dusters made from ostrich plumes.

Hunters chased the ostrich flocks, certain they would make their fortunes. Plucking feathers from a wild ostrich is risky business, however. One kick can kill a man. Knowing that, the plume hunters shot the birds instead of trying to capture them. The killing went on and on. Soon there were no ostriches to be found in North Africa, Egypt, Persia, and Arabia.

Ostrich farms save the species

The ostrich was saved by farmers. Instead of hunting the birds, a South African started the first ostrich farm in 1838. The fierce ostrich turned out to be quite tame when it was hatched and raised in captivity. When farmers cut or plucked the feathers carefully, the ostriches lived to grow a new crop. In addition to South Africa, ostrich farms opened in Algeria, Sicily, France, Germany, Florida, and Australia. Later, many of the Australian birds were set free. As a result, southern Australia still has a population of wild ostriches.

Selling ostrich feathers became a big business. A good breeding cock sold for $7,500 (US) just before World War I. That was equal to the price of ten Ford Model T's! By this time, South Africa was exporting over 800,000 pounds (362,880 kg) of feathers each year.

After World War I, women stopped wearing hats and carrying fans. The price of ostrich feathers dropped and ostrich hunters turned to other game. Many ostrich farmers went broke.

Today, ostrich farms have made a comeback. The farms in the Oudtshoorn district of South Africa keep ninety thousand ostriches. The farmers sell the feathers, eat ostrich steaks, and tan the hides for wallets and boots. A large ostrich yields twenty-one square feet (2 sq. m) of hide. In addition, each cock produces two pounds (.9 kg) of feathers every nine months. A pound of plumes is now worth about $70 (US).

The ostriches also attract tourists. Gentle birds are harnessed to a dogcart to entertain the children. The farmers also put on ostrich races. The jockeys sit high on the birds' backs and steer by tugging at their wings.

Ostrich farmers in South Africa enjoy an unusual sporting event: ostrich racing!

Tourists are allowed to take a ride, but they usually fall off. At lunchtime, the cook serves ostrich-egg omelettes.

Whether you see ostriches on a farm or at the zoo, no one is allowed to feed them. The birds will eat almost anything they can get their beaks on. These "snacks" have included rings, keys, pocketknives, and coins. A few ostriches have died after swallowing sharp, shiny objects. In one case, an ostrich drank a pail of green paint.

Can the ostrich survive?

Over 750,000 ostriches once lived in a single province of South Africa. Today, there are less than 150,000 ostriches left in the entire world. Except for the Northern ostrich, the species isn't endangered. Naturalists worry, however, that wild ostriches may soon disappear. Except in the game preserves, ostrich habitat is giving way to human settlement. Several subspecies have been lost already.

Will the ostrich become extinct, as did the moa and the elephant bird? Those people lucky enough to have seen this largest of all living birds—and those still waiting for the chance—hope that won't happen.

MAP:

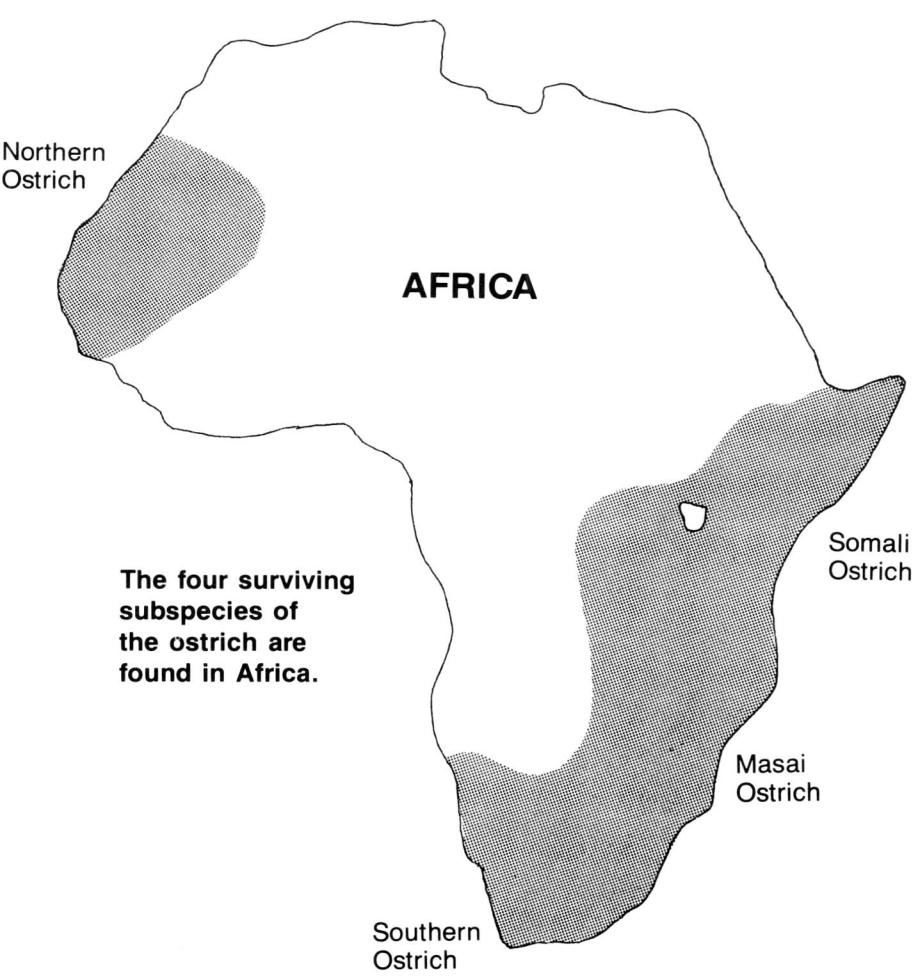

INDEX/GLOSSARY:

BEHAVIOR 12, 16, 21, 30, 32, 36, 39

CARINATES 8, 11 — *Birds that have the ability to fly.*

CHICK 11, 16, 17, 20, 26, 29, 30, 32, 35, 36, 39 — *A young male or female ostrich.*

CLUTCH 34 — *All the eggs found in an ostrich nest.*

COCK 14, 15, 16, 18, 20, 23, 26, 29, 30, 33, 34, 36, 39, 42, 43 — *An adult male ostrich.*

COLOR 16, 17, 36

DIET 20, 26, 28, 36

DISPLAY 16, 33 — *The ritual behaviors a male ostrich goes through when it's courting a hen or trying to frighten another cock.*

DOWN 36 — *The soft, fluffy feathers of an ostrich chick.*

ENDANGERED SPECIES 45 — *An animal that is in danger of becoming extinct.*

ENEMIES 29, 36, 37, 41, 42

EXTINCTION 9, 14, 41, 45 — *The loss of a species, as when the last animal of that species dies.*

GAME PRESERVE 41, 45 — *A protected area where wild animals can live naturally and safely.*

GIZZARD 20, 21, 27 — *An enlarged section of the ostrich's intestines, where grit and small stones aid in digestion.*

HABITAT 14, 17, 23, 26, 32, 45 — *The place where an animal makes its home.*

IMPRINTING 35 — *The process by which a newly hatched ostrich chick learns to recognize its parents by sight and sound.*

INCUBATE 30 — *To keep eggs warm in order to hatch them.*

INSTINCT 26, 36 — *Behaviors an animal knows from the time it's born.*

MAJOR HEN 33, 34 — *An ostrich cock's primary mate. Only the major hen is allowed to sit on the nest.*

MATING 33, 39, 40

INDEX/GLOSSARY:

MINOR HEN 33, 34, 35 — *An ostrich hen that hasn't found a primary mate. Minor hens mate with many different cocks and lay their eggs in several different nests.*

NATURALIST 8, 9, 11, 14, 19, 21, 23, 27, 30, 32, 35, 45 — *A scientist who studies animals and plants.*

PHYSICAL CHARACTERISTICS 11, 12, 14, 16, 17, 19, 20, 37, 39

PLUMES 16, 33, 39, 41, 42, 43 — *Large, fluffy white feathers on the wings and tail that the cock uses as part of his display.*

PREDATORS 12, 23, 26, 28, 29, 30, 35, 36, 37 — *Animals that live by preying on other animals.*

RATITES 8, 9, 11 — *Birds that have lost the ability to fly.*

SAVANNAH 26, 28 — *A flat, treeless African grassland.*

SCAVENGER 30 — *An animal that feeds on the dead bodies of other animals.*

SENSES 19, 22, 23
SIZE 14, 19, 30, 36, 37
SOUNDS 23, 33, 35, 36, 40
WEIGHT 14, 30

READ AND ENJOY THE SERIES:

If you would like to know more about all kinds of wildlife, you should take a look at the other books in this series.

You'll find books on bald eagles and other birds. Books on alligators and other reptiles. There are books about deer and other big-game animals. And there are books about sharks and other creatures that live in the ocean.

In all of the books you will learn that life in the wild is not easy. But you will also learn what people can do to help wildlife survive. So read on!